IT'S NOTHING BUT GIBBERISH

PAMELA TUCKER

Copyright © 2020 by Pamela Tucker

All rights reserved. No part of this publication may be reproduced, distributed , or transmitted in any form or by any means , including photocopying , recording, or other electronic or mechanical methods , without the prior written permission of the publisher,except in the case of brief quotations embodied in critical reviews and certain other non commercial uses permitted by copyright law. For permission requests, write to the publisher , and Author addressed "Attention : Permissions Coordinator" at the address below

"Scriptures references are taken from the New International Version unless otherwise stated".

Printed in the United States of America

First Printing, 2020

ISBN: 978-1-7350031-0-8

Email: ReStartenterprise2017@gmail.com

DEDICATION

*First, I thank God for His grace, mercy,
and strength to complete this book without God none
of this would have been possible.*

*I would like to dedicate this book
to the people who will read it.
Be careful with your words.*

It will change someone's life.

ACKNOWLEDGMENTS

To my Blessed Family

*My Daughters, Olivia, Antiea,
Breanna, and my precious grandbaby Peyton.*

My siblings Mary, Jimmy, Brenda

Also to my Friends

*Thank you all for your prayers
and support, push, and encouragement.*

I love you all.

TABLE OF CONTENTS

INTRODUCTION 6

CHAPTER 1: NOT GOOD ENOUGH 8

CHAPTER 2: THE SHAME 14

CHAPTER 3: WHY CAN'T I BE 22

CHAPTER 4: DOCTOR SAY, BUT GOD SAID 27

CHAPTER 5: THE CHATTER 31

CHAPTER 6: WORDS CAN KILL 34

CHAPTER 7: I AM NOT 37

GIBBERISH RAP 39

BE CAREFUL WITH YOUR WORDS 40

O.P.O 42

ABOUT THE AUTHOR 44

PRAYER 45

INTRODUCTION

It is true that no man is an island. We are surrounded by people who are supposed to care and understand us as to make contributions in our lives. Sometimes, these people have earned our loyalty and have the greatest influence in our lives. Our Parents, Family members, Friends, Teachers, Doctors, associates and yes, even Pastors, make the list.

We go through life believing what others have said about us. Some people fail to search inside of themselves to discover the internal yearning of their hearts and the power within them. On a second thought, it could be that the voice of the people on the outside is louder than the whispers of the interior man. Many people have given up on starting a business, marriage, writing, singing, and so many other different things in life, because of some discouraging words someone said.

That's Nothing but Gibberish.

Some things we have heard have been nothing but nonsense. We will tell you stories about different things that has happened all because of someone's gibberish.

Don't allow someone's gibberish to define who God said you are.

CHAPTER 1

NOT GOOD ENOUGH

Early on one Tuesday morning, my phone rang. It was Max, a young man that I spoke with a year ago, about a situation. Ever since then, he would call me every month just for us to catch up on what was going on in his life.

This particular Tuesday call was for a different issue all together. Max was in my town, and he wanted us to meet at Gouda Upscale café at 12noon? I said, "Max, if it's the Lord's will, I can meet you at 12:15pm. Is that okay?" He said yes. So, we fixed the appointment and I was expecting to hear a follow-up on his life as usual.

I went into the café, and was telling them who I was looking for. Before I could finish, Max came up and said, "Hey Ms.

Kamille," with a broad grin that is rather unusual of his attitude, and gave me a big hug. I said, "hi Max." After exchanging some pleasantries, He led the way to another dining area. He pulled out my chair. I said thank you. When he sat down, I said, "Max, you look like something is happening, and it smells good, whatever it may be." He said, "Ms. Kamille, I have something to show you. The last time we saw each other was on mobile facetime, but this time I wanted to meet with you in person. I said okay with a smile on my face, but the grin on his own face was very large.

Max excused himself for a short time. When he came back, he had a young lady and she was holding a little baby. He said, "Ms. Kamille, this is my wife, Beth, and this is our daughter,

Joy." I was glad to meet them and I stood up to hug his wife and their bundle of joy. When we all sat down, Max introduced me to his wife and shared with her how we both met. Max began to take a trip down memory lane. He began to share for the first time, everything that had happened and how him and I started talking.

Max started: "I heard about Ms. Kamille from Tom at church. He said Ms. Kamille is a great listener, and I was really going through something that I could not face any longer." Max's eyes became teary. So, I took the narrative from him and said to Beth, "this is how it all happened. I had a phone conference with somebody named Max, a 27-year-old man. We were to talk about him getting married to the pastor's daughter. I was very happy to listen to him. So, for the first 20 minutes, I listened to him talk about how he was unsure if he could provide for his fiancé. He was so confused about what he wanted and what he should be doing. He went as far to say that he didn't think he wanted any kids, but she wanted 3, two boys and a girl.

When he finished speaking, I said, 'Max, does your fiancée know how you feel?' He said no. I could tell that someone had been in Max ear, so I asked, 'have you spoken to anyone before now about your concerns?' He said yes, to her dad. Okay, what did you share with him? He said, 'I told him that I love his daughter, and I would like to marry his daughter.' Her dad asked, 'Son, where do you work?' At a warehouse, Max replied. The Pastor said, 'I will not prolong this meeting. This is what you need before you can marry my daughter.' Max said.

He gave him a list of things he needs to have before he comes back to speak to him.

Max confided in me that he really loves the girl and he knew she loves him too, but he can't do a lot of the things her dad was asking of him. Max shared a few of the things the Pastor was demanding. It reads,

To the man that wants to marry my daughter. You must have and do the following things.

1. You have to join my church
2. You have to make at least 80,000 + a year
3. You have to own your home at least 5 bedrooms 4 baths
4. You will have to have 2 kids, a boy and a girl.

Max said with frustration, 'Ms. Kamille, you see what I am talking about? I won't tell you what he said about the tithes. All of this is nothing but GIBBERISH. Who tells someone to have those things, and if he doesn't, he cannot marry his daughter? I don't know what to do. I think I'm just going to give up, and tell her I can't marry her.,

I was just listening to him, and I could hear his hurt. Then he was getting ready to say something, but the Holy Spirit in me spoke up and said, 'you will not kill yourself.' He burst out screaming. I began to pray and call on the name of Jesus, pleading the blood of Jesus over Max. Then his screaming turned into a deep cry. I could feel his pain that I wept with him. He took a moment to get himself together.

He tried to apologize, but I declined it because he needed to get that out, for the healing process to start.

He said, 'how did you know I was thinking about taking my life?' I respond that the Holy Spirit knows all things. I began to tell him what the Holy Spirit was saying to me about him, and what he should do in this situation. He was to talk to his fiancée and both of them were to fast and pray together in agreement for 3 days for what they are believing God to do for them.

Both of them are believers in the body of Christ Jesus. They trust and believe in God. But Max had been weakened in the spirit already by the words he was told. He said, I don't think God loves me anymore. I stopped praying because I didn't think he heard me anymore.'

Max said he's been carrying those emotions for months and no one knew it. He said, 'then I speak to a total stranger, and God spoke to me. It's a sign that God still Loves me after all.'

Max started crying again but this time, it was tears of joy. The love of Jesus Christ has wrapped his loving arms around him. I could feel it too.

I exclaimed, 'God is good' and he replied, 'yes HE is All the time.' I said, 'I'm going to ask you to pray, Max, but before you do, I just want to say that it was a pleasure speaking with you. I will be praying for you. Let me know when you and your fiancée get married. May God bless you and stay wrapped in the love of Jesus' arms. Please Pray.' Max prayed and the conversation was done."

I hung up from max and began to think how many times a Pastor/Leader has told a person or people something that was not of God that has caused them to stop hoping and even believing in God. Some people may have been like Max in some ways even to the point of giving up on fellowship, life, for some, even giving up on God all because of what a pastor /leader has said or even done to them.

People might have caused you to think differently about yourself, and about God because of the words they have spoken over you. I want to uplift someone with the word of God today. That is not what God's word says about you. You have no reason to despair or become despondent. Rise up and dust yourself, for God is speaking success into all your endeavors.

Romans 8:31 (NIV)

What, then, shall we say in response to these things? If God is for us, who can be against us?

Proverbs 3:5-6 Trust in the LORD with all your heart and do not lean on your own understanding. In all your ways acknowledge him ,and he will direct your paths.

CHAPTER 2

THE SHAME

My friend Julie and I decided to go on a road trip to the beach for the weekend. We had so much fun, laughing, singing, telling jokes, and reminiscing on our better days ago. I remember moments when the bus was 25cents, when we could stop and use a pay phone for a 10cent, or when we used to catch lightning bugs in a jar.

What about church every Friday? It was either condensed prayer sessions or a revival. Something was always going on at the church at least 5 days out of the seven. In those days, the church was always open. If you needed prayer, or baptism, or you just needed to talk, someone was always around to attend to your spiritual needs.

We missed those days but we had to stop reminiscing, and asked ourselves, "what happened to the church?"

After a few stops, a fill-up, and lots of laughs, we arrived at the beach. We got out of the car and headed to the ocean. We stood in the water as the waves were coming in strong. We held on to each other so we would not be taken into the ocean by the waves. Later, we stepped out of the water and went to sit in the beach chairs as we gazed at the waves and other people playing in the water having fun.

Julie said to me, "Kamille, would you like to know why I left the church?" It has been 5years since Julie left the place we worshiped. I didn't really know what to say. I answered by asking her if she feels like sharing it? She responded with a yes. So, I listened.

She said when she found out that she was pregnant, she went to speak with one of the church leaders to let them know before it starts showing really good and to get some advice. When she was finished talking, the leader told her that she was going to hell with her baby, because she was not married. She said she could not pray for her, and that she needs to find another church to attend because God hates that kind of sin. With that, the leader walked out of their meeting.

She said Kamille, "I sat there thinking, 'Lord, forgive me please don't send me and my baby to hell, I'm sorry' where can

I go? What other church can I attend like this? I left there more confused than when I came. I was crying so hard that I could not drive. Everything that the leader said played over in my mind that I started believing everything that was said about me; all the negative words that had been spoken over me made me feel ashamed, humiliated and unloved. It may not have hit me so hard if it was from somebody that I did not know, but this was someone that had influence over me. I respected and loved this person. I left there thinking that God does not love me nor my baby anymore, all because of what I did. I went back to whoever would take me and show me any kind of love. My heart felt shattered, I couldn't even pray because I didn't think God would hear me. Kamille, I went from this man to that man, searching for someone to love me, but I did not love myself. I had forgotten what love was and even how it felt. I changed my phone number because I did not want to be bothered by the so-called church people. After about 5 years, my life changed and I have 4 kids now.

One day, I stumbled on an old email you sent me. I remember exactly what it said,

Hey Julie, Letting you know that I miss you; I have been praying for you. Talk to God, He's waiting. He Loves you Julie. God Bless, Love Kamille.

You sent me this same email about 20 times within those years, but that was my first time seeing it. I am not sure why it happened like that, but that day I really needed those words. From that point on, I talked with God and He spoke back to me. I asked God to forgive me, I repented of all my sins.

After that I felt so free and so much love. All I could say was, 'thank you Jesus for loving me.' I started screaming, 'Jesus loves me....' My kids ran into the room. 'You okay, Mom?' I could not answer. The Holy Spirit had filled my mouth. Oh, what joy that floods my soul. God changed me, Kamille. I can't really explain everything. I am so grateful for your email. God placed me in a church that sees what God has placed in me and my kids. They're nurturing us, and helping us to grow in the word and knowledge of God. Prayer is everything. My intimate time with Jesus is everything to me; even my kids have an intimate time with Jesus."

"So, Kamille, that's what happened," she concluded. Tears rolled down my cheeks and so did Julie's. We got up and hugged each other and wiped our tears away. All I could say at that moment was, "WOW!! GOD!!!"

We stood there in silence listening to the ocean waves, and looking at the bluish-green beauty of the water. Julie said we need to go and settle in and relax for a few minutes before we go get some dinner. We walked away singing, *HE Touched Me,*

Oh HE Touched Me, What Joy That Flooded Our Souls. We had a moment of praising and worshiping God right at the beach. What a mighty God we serve.

We finally left the beach to go check into a hotel, but to my surprise, Julie said, 'I have something to show you, Kamille.' About 10 minutes' drive from the beach, she pulled up to this gated-house, keyed in a code, and drove right in. She parked the car, got out and shouted, surprise!!! What surprise, Julie? She said we are staying here for the weekend. "Oh, wow, great," I replied, but I got a feeling that there is something more to this house. I held it to myself. With a grin on my face, we went in.

"What a magnificent house." Julie said thank you. She said it's Five bedrooms upstairs and three downstairs, and asked which would I prefer. I said let me go check them all out and see which one meets my needs, and wants for the weekend. She was flipping the TV sitting in an oversize chair. As I went to the different rooms, all of them were enormous and pristine. They all have what I needed, but only three have what I wanted: a Jacuzzi tub, a steam shower, and so much more. When I chose the bed room I wanted for the weekend, I told Julie. She said, "okay, let's get ready for dinner then, or would you like to stay in and freestyle? Hmm, let's see what's in the refrigerator all you have to do is speak to it."

What? Speak to the refrigerator? So, I said, "what type of meat do you have?" This refrigerator answered, "hey" and began to list the meat, veggies, fruit, breads, snacks etc. it had inside of it.

I was amazed beyond words. "Okay, Julie, whose house is this?" She said, "Kamille, we have known each other for years now. You know I was always told that I would not be anything nor would I have anything. Kamille I remember when you asked me what I wanted, and I said to have favor with God and man. You prayed for me right there and then, and you said something about a home that was beautiful. This is one of the homes I own."

Julie was so grateful to God for all He had done and is doing in her family life. We caught up on so many other things we went up on the third deck where you can see the ocean and the sunset.

I was lost for words. It was marvelous, looking at the resplendence of the sunset over the bluish-green ocean.

Julie and I were eating some fruits, and veggies, while discussing. What an awesome conversation. I will share just a little.

Julie began to tell me about some words of abuse she received. It made no sense to her why it was happening at that moment. She went on to say that a lot of the negative words that were spoken over her, were said by people that said they loved Jesus. In her words, "they came against my life, my children and so much more."

She said she began to cry one Sunday during service and God spoke to her directly. "I got you my child; all will be well. I will fight for you." Then the Pastor got up and beckoned on her, "Sister Julie, you and your children come to the altar please." When they got to the altar, he asked the mothers and the elders of the church to come and pray for them. They prayed against every negative word spoken over me, and every secret hurt, shame, pain, confusion, abuse, misuse, doubt, double mindedness, anxiety, self-hatred, anger, madness, unforgiveness, jealousy, secret sin, fornication, suicide, just to name a few. There were so much more.

She said, "The Pastor could not preach, the Holy Spirit had taken over. We were all prostrated out before God, crying out for forgiveness, Repenting. We were drunk in the spirit; asking for more of Jesus Christ.

After that event, my life and my children's lives changed. "Wow, God. You did it again, that's all I could say." I was just in awe with what God was doing for her, and her family. We went to the theater room and sat down. She spoke to the movie to start, and it did. The title of the movie was "*IT'S NOTHING*

BUT GIBBERISH." God turned every negative word into a positive movie for her and her family.

I had to share these stories because oftentimes we go through life with the negative words of someone else in our ears. Sometimes, we allow those words to define us, to make and even stop us from moving forward. We should depend on what God has spoken, and still speaks over us. I hope this frees you to trust what God has said and is saying about you. Believe and Trust God.

Matthew 6:14 (NIV)

For if you forgive other people when they sin against you, your Heavenly Father will also forgive you.

1 Peter 5:10 After you have suffered for a while, the God of all grace, who called you to His eternal glory in Christ , will Himself perfect , confirm, strengthen, and establish you.

CHAPTER 3

WHY CAN'T I BE

Have you ever been told that you couldn't do or be something when you were growing up? And when you became an adult those very words were still attached to you? My friend, Eunice, and I were talking and she shared some words that had been spoken over her as a child that she thought were gone when she got older but she realized that those words were still with her.

When she was little she would tell her parents that she wanted to be a Doctor when she grew up. They would look at her, and say, "you are not doctor material." She said her heart was broken to hear what her parents said to her and she wanted to know what type of material she had to be to be a doctor? She asked her dad, "why can't I be a doctor?" He answered her, "we told you why already. You don't have the right material."

She said, "kamille, I just walked away with the question in my mind, 'why am I not the right material?'"

I said, "Eunice, did you ever ask what material?" She recounted another event that broke her the more. One evening, members of the family were watching TV, and a commercial came on. It was about joining the Navy. Her brother William said that is what he was going to be when he grew up. Her parents said, "oh, that would be nice, William, a Navy man."

They were talking about it like he was already in the Navy. I sat there quietly, thinking to myself, "I want to be a doctor, and they tell me that I don't have the right material, but William says he is joining the Navy when he gets older, and the celebration began." My mom said, "Eunice, did you hear your brother? What do you think?"

She said, "Kamille, before I knew it, I bared my mind, 'I don't think he has the right material!'" Her dad jumped up, and said, "William can be a Navy man. It's not hard, and besides, he will be a man soon."

Eunice went to bed with the thought that boys can be, or even do more than girls. What was said that night puzzled her mind. She needed to ask them again because she was confused.

So, she got out of bed and asked her parents why William could join the Navy but she can't be a doctor. "Eunice, you have a speech problem, and you are in special classes for speech. How can you be a doctor? We don't want to hear anything else about you wanting to be a doctor. Now go to bed."

Eunice said she went to bed crying because she still didn't understand what her speech problem had to do with her wanting to be a doctor.

She said as she grew up, she felt like she could not be what she wanted to be because of what her parents said to her that night.

I said, "Eunice, what made you share your story now with me?" She said, "when I was a teenager, and you and I were talking, I told you I wanted to be a doctor but I couldn't, because of my speech problem. You looked at me, and said, 'that's gibberish. Why can't you be a doctor? You can do all things through Christ that strengthens you.' Then you said, Eunice, I believe in you, and you walked away."

"That changed my life, Kamille. You said you believed in me, and there I was feeling sorry for myself. I had to stop feeling sorry for myself and started believing in myself. I had to tell myself that what my parents were telling me was nothing but gibberish. It took years to remove that nonsense (gibberish) from my mind. When I did, I graduated from High School and went straight to college, staying focused on my dream.

Not only did I start working on my dream, but I received the Lord Jesus Christ as my savior. That was the Greatest thing that could have ever happened to me, and I am so grateful to God. I pray before going out the door every day. I always said a prayer before I took any test. Other students would be watching me. To my surprise, they asked if we all could pray together. From that day on, we started praying together until graduation.

Kamille, not only did God allow me to complete medical school and become a Doctor at the top of my class. All of that is good but the miracle is that God healed me. I don't have a speech problem at all. I didn't realize until I had to speak in front of the MD board and I prayed to God to help me not to be nervous that I may speak right In Jesus Name."

"Wow Eunice that is a remarkable testimony." She said that now, when people are saying things that don't make sense to her, she would just say that's nothing but gibberish. She said everywhere she goes, she tells people to trust God, to listen to Him, and to develop a relationship with HIM that they may know what He has said about them so they won't receive any gibberish nor fluff in their lives.

"Kamille, I just wanted to share a little of my testimony, and to say thank you for believing in me. I attend to so many people with health issues. I am passionate about helping them, but I first encourage them in their minds to believe and trust God for their healing.

I encourage anyone that God has placed a dream in you of being something great but all you have around you is naysayers speaking gibberish in your ears.

I want to encourage you like I was encouraged, to believe in yourself and the dreams that God has given you, and allow God to lead and guide you to your destiny which He has prepared for you. If God is saying you can do it, then, you can do it. If HE says you can be it, then, you can be it. God will back it up. I am a witness to that.

Mark 10:27 (NIV) Jesus looked at them and said , "With man this is impossible , but not with God, all things are possible with God."

Numbers 23:19 (KJV)

God is not a man, that he should lie; neither the son of man, that he should repent: hath he said, and shall he not do it? or hath he spoken, and shall he not make it good?

CHAPTER 4

DOCTOR SAY, BUT GOD SAID

I met my friend George at the library. We have not seen each other in a long while. It was so good to see him while we were at the library catching up on old times. George started to get a certain kind of frown gesture on his face and he began to share with me what happened with his dad.

He said, "Mille, that's what he called me , my dad was going to the doctors, specialists, and the hospitals for about 3 months. No one knew what was wrong with him. He was losing weight and he was off-balance and tripping. George said that to see his dad go from a strong built firm man who worked-out with him 5 times a week to a man who needed help going to the restroom, and help feeding him was devastating to me George said.

"I carried him around to see many Doctors and specialists to no avail. We eventually ended up at a hospital that had a doctor who knew exactly what was wrong with my dad. She was a straightforward doctor. She said to my dad, 'you have a rare infection called septicemia, and I can't help you. It is too far gone.' She sent my dad home. She said I should keep him comfortable and handed me some pain killers for him."

I revolted against the idea of sending him home because he was in excruciating pain. The Doctor turned around and said there was nothing she could do. My dad held me back from following the Doctor and said, "son, take me home. I know another Doctor we should try."

Hearing my dad moaning and groaning left me in tears and asking God why. To cut the long story short, I asked my dad about the other doctor when I got him home and into bed.

I asked my dad, "does this Doctor make house calls? What is the number so I can call him to come first thing in the morning.

"Mille," my dad said, "the doctor gave me her opinion just like the others. Now, I am going to get God's opinion. I should have done this in the first place. He said, son, I will let you know how I am in the morning. I got to talk with my Father. Close the door behind you, he said.

George said, "I heard my dad praying like he used to. Then I heard him moaning and groaning but there was something different about it this time. The next morning, I knocked on my dad's door. His voice was so weak. I went in and said, "dad, how are you feeling this morning? My dad just nodded his head ``What can I get you to eat this morning."

"My dad was looking worse to me. I fought back tears. I knew he could see it in my face. He said, "son, get me these items." I got my pen; I wrote down what he said. He only named two items. I said, "dad, that's only 2 things. Is there nothing else?" He said, "no, son, that's it." I went and got those items and came right back.

The library was about to close. We went outside and continued because I wanted to hear this story to the end. We went outside and stood by my car, while he finished with his story. He said "Mille, the next 7 days with my dad changed my life."

"My dad started doing something three times every day, and he asked me to do it with him, and I did. For seven days, I tended my dad to the restroom, and fed him as usual.

Now, my dad gets up on his own and goes to the restroom and feeds himself. He made his closet into a prayer closet for him and God. I saw God work miracles not only in my dad's life, but in mine too.

I received the LORD JESUS CHRIST as my savior. My dad was healed. That same doctor who told us my dad's condition was helpless said, "I am not sure what you have done, but you are as fit as a fiddle." I said, "Wow, God you did it again. Thank you, Jesus."

Before we left, I said, "George, what did your dad do to get well?" He replied, "He called Jehovah Rapha - The LORD who heals you. God told my dad what to do and scriptures to pray with. To this day, my dad still says those scriptures and takes communion every day, and so do I."

I thanked George for sharing his dad's testimony with me, and his salvation. It was amazing. Only God has the final say in our lives. Every discouragement from anyone is nothing but gibberish.

Jeremiah 17:14 Heal me, O LORD, and I will be healed ; save me and I will be saved, for You are my praise.

Luke 15:10 (NIV)

In the same way, I tell you, there is rejoicing in the presence of the angels of God over one sinner who repents."

CHAPTER 5

THE CHATTER

Mr. Benjamin and I were having a great conversation. Whenever I speak with this man, it feels like I'm in elementary school all over again. This man has such great and rare wisdom, so I mostly listen and take notes. Mr. Benjamin said that something has happened to the church, and it has changed in a way that is not good. He begin to tell me how it was back in his day he was born in 1933 he said he received the LORD Jesus Christ as his savior at the age of 10 years old

He said they were on one accord. Mr. Benjamin said they were excited about what God did every time they got together. I saw so many miracles that God performed where we met.

"Did you all ever have a church building?" I asked. "We did, but something would happen to them. But it did not stop us from worshipping God. We would meet in the cellar or in the woods. We were hungry for the word of God, but now the people are so weak-minded about Fellowship. They are paying attention to worldly things, fleshly things more than to God. They depend on man, woman ,job and money more than God."

He said Kamille "We were once invited to a particular church to worship the Lord. When we got there, a lady at the entrance said we had to wait outside because they were behind time; they were late opening the building, their church building. While we waited, the people started complaining. They were murmuring and grumbling on different issues. One of the men told another, 'I better have my seat on the second row, or else I am leaving.' Someone else said, 'I hope the camera gets me today.' The other person replied to him, 'just start shouting; they will put the camera right on you,' and smacked his lips.

A lady said to her friend, "I need God to speak to me." Then her friend responded by saying, "at the end of the service, they will ask for what I call 'special money'. Just have your money ready because when they call out that amount, and you have it, and give it, you will get your word from God.

Kamille, I could not believe my ears and the blather it was taking in from the people around me. I thought to myself, 'this is gibberish.'"

Eventually, the lady came out, and said the doors are now open. The people were pushing to get inside. They were about to knock a few of us elderly people down without apology, pardon me, or sorry. I will not talk about how the rite was, but one thing that bothers me is all the chatter about Mazuma.

Kamille, I did not hear anyone ask the people do you have a need today it could have been people hungry and they let them leave. What happened to us helping one another. It's time to go back to the basics. Kamille will end our conversation after this. Understand that some words that are being told to us are nothing but Gibberish.

Matthew 6:24 (NIV)

24 "No one can serve two masters. Either you will hate the one and love the other, or you will be devoted to the one and despise the other. You cannot serve both God and money.

2 Peter 1:21 (KJV)

For the prophecy came not in old time by the will of man: but holy men of God spake as they were moved by the Holy Ghost.

CHAPTER 6

WORDS CAN KILL

I was out walking at Yellowstone Park, I heard someone call my name Kamille they said is that you? I stopped and looked to see a person running toward me from a distance. I see him. It's my old classmate Charlie from middle school. We have not seen each other in over 10 years. He moved during the school year. He comes up to me and hugs me by surprise.

We went to sit down on the bench as we talked about old times catching each other up with what's been going on in each other's lives.

We were talking about other classmates and the teacher we had and some things we used to do. I asked him about Stan, his best friend and he looked kind of sad; he said Kamille, Stan died 3mos ago. I said I'm sorry to hear that, I know how close you and Stan were.

Jay said Stan killed himself and left a letter behind. In his letter, he said this, Sticks and Stones may break your bones but names /words will never hurt you he said that is GIBBERISH, names/ words hurt a matter of fact they can kill.

It kills your will, your emotions, your mindset. It even kills your will to live. My wife told me I was nothing because I could not afford to buy her a new Rolls-Royce Sweptail, she wanted. She told me to just die.

I will miss you all but I want to give my wife what she asked for. This is for you, my darling wife. I Could not afford that car but I will die for you.

If you can imagine the look on my face. I was lost for words for a moment then I said how is the wife? He said the last he heard she had a mental breakdown.

"Jay went on to say Kamille, some people are so mean that they don't care about one other like they used to. Some only care about themselves; they say a lot of hurtful words. Those words have caused someone to stop living their life and now they are just existing with no hope, no dreams and no desires.

He said after that happened to Stan he started traveling the world telling people to let their words Heal and not Kill.

Proverbs 18:21 (MSG) Words kill, Words give life; they're either poison or fruit you choose.

Psalm 141:3 (NIV) Set a guard over my mouth, Lord; keep watch over the door of my lips.

CHAPTER 7

I AM NOT

- I Am Not Stupid
- I Am Not Dumb
- I Am Not Bad
- I Am Not Ugly
- I Am Not Foolish
- I Am Not Irresponsible
- I Am Not Incompitent
- I Am Not Weird
- I Am Not Fearful
- I Am Not Hated
- I Am Not Shy
- I Am Not Useless
- I Am Not Inferior

▲ I Am Not A Failure

Gibberish here Gibberish there do you think gibberish care?

There are so many words that have been spoken over you or someone you care about. If someone is speaking these words all the time it begins to take root in a person's mind even in their life. If you don't come against it and cast it out of your mind.

Don't allow any negative words to define you. Understand who God said and is saying you are.

Remember you are Fearfully and Wonderfully made by God, not only that God made you in HIS image..

Psalm 139:14 (NIV) I praise you because I am fearfully and wonderfully made; Your works are wonderful, I know that full well.

Genesis 1:27 (NIV) So God created mankind in his own image, in the image of God created them; male and female he created them.

GIBBERISH RAP

I heard to men say oh boy what a good day someone else came along and started singing this song it went like this blah blah blah---- blah blah blah oh oh oh blah blah blah oh blah blah well the two guys said man we don't understand anything you said break it down right so he said its nothing but gibberish is what he said; I held your attention for as long as I want singing a song that didn't make no sense. How many times have y'all done this, Give attention to words that don't make any sense blah blah blah How many times have you done this sit listening to words that are nonsense Gibberish, Gibberish is the words I say that's all yall have a nice day.

BE CAREFUL WITH YOUR WORDS

I believe words are more important than we really know because if we really knew how important words were we would be careful what we say to each other and ourselves and the way we say it. God was meticulous when He spoke everything into existence with words. What God spoke brought life into a dark place.

What words are you speaking into someone?
Does it bring life or death to a person?
Be careful what comes out of your mouth.
Ephesians (NIV) 4:29

29 Do not let any unwholesome talk come out of your mouths, but only what is helpful for building others up according to their needs, that it may benefit those who listen.

O.P.O

We go through this life asking other people's opinions in different areas of our lives, whether it's about a hairstyle, outfits, makeup, haircut, choice of vehicle, house, marriage, raising children, what to eat, what to drink, what to watch, best vacation, best school, business moves, health, weather, even our salvation.

It's okay sometimes to ask these questions and more. But understand that this is just other people's opinions, it's not written in stone. Sometimes, it's not based on facts nor knowledge. It's just what a person thinks it should be for you and your life.

We cannot deny that other people's opinions can be good, But, what is your opinion about yourself? What do you think

God has to say in your situation? Ultimately, all that matters is what you believe about yourself, and what God says. Any other opposing opinion is nothing but gibberish.

ABOUT THE AUTHOR

Pamela Tucker is an advocate for the forgotten. Her heart for people and efforts to help others live their best life has made her an active humanitarian.

She has three daughters and one granddaughter Pamela is the author of the books Forgive Me Forgive Me Not Vols 1 & 2 , and Why Are You Broke When You Say You Know Jesus Pamela resides in metro Atlanta where she lives a life of Forgiveness.

PRAYER

Father God in the name of Jesus, I forgive those who spoke any gibberish or writings of nonsense to me . I repent of the gibberish that I allowed to come out of my mouth and even what has entered my mind and my ears, forgive me,

I come against every wrong thinking and every wrong speaking transform my thoughts and let me understand how fearfully and wonderfully you made me.

Transform my speaking and let me speak what you have spoken over me.

Father allow my words to heal, not kill.

I now speak Hope, Favor, Peace, Wealth, Integrity, Kindness, Health, Compassion, Strength. Boldness, and Love of God upon my life.

In Jesus' name, Amen

www.ingramcontent.com/pod-product-compliance
Lightning Source LLC
Chambersburg PA
CBHW071802040426
42446CB00012B/2681